WEAVING YOUR TAPESTRY

UNLEASHING YOUR INNER CREATOR

FATEMA KAPADIA

Made with ♥ on the Notion Press Platform
www.notionpress.com

To the sunshine of my life , my husband and daughter , who lights up my world,

Your love , a gentle rain,

Nourishes my world and makes my dream bloom.

-fatema kapadia

Contents

Contents

Contents

Foreword

Preface

Weaving Your Tapestry: Unleashing Your Inner Creator

In the quiet corners of our minds, a vibrant tapestry awaits to be woven. Threads of imagination, patience, and thought intertwine, forming intricate patterns that reflect the unique essence of our souls. This book invites you to embark on a journey of self-discovery, where you will learn to harness the power of words and the artistry of creation.

Within these pages, you will find a compass to guide you through the labyrinth of your thoughts. You will learn to cultivate patience, a virtue that allows your ideas to mature and your creativity to flourish. By honing your thinking skills, you will unlock the door to a world of endless possibilities.

As you delve deeper into this exploration, you will

discover the transformative power of words. They are the tools with which we shape our reality, express our emotions, and inspire others. By mastering the art of wordplay, you will learn to communicate your thoughts with clarity and eloquence.

Remember, the tapestry of your life is a masterpiece in progress. With each stroke of your pen and each thought you ponder, you are adding to its beauty and complexity. Embrace the journey, trust your intuition, and let your inner creator shine.

Acknowledgements

As I embark on this journey of sharing my thoughts and experiences, I am deeply grateful for the unwavering support and encouragement of those who have made this book possible.

First and foremost, I want to express my heartfelt gratitude to my beloved husband,whose love, patience, and belief in me have been an endless source of inspiration. Your unwavering support has given me the strength to pursue my dreams and share my passions with the world.

To my dear daughter your boundless creativity and infectious enthusiasm have ignited a spark within me. Your curiosity and imagination have been a constant reminder of the beauty and wonder that exists within us all.

I would also like to extend my sincere thanks to Notion Press for their invaluable guidance and support throughout the publication process. Your team's professionalism and dedication have made this journey smoother and more enjoyable.

Finally, I am eternally grateful to the countless individuals who have crossed my path, inspiring and uplifting me along the way. Your wisdom, kindness, and encouragement have shaped me into the person I am today.

Thank you all for being a part of this extraordinary tapestry.

Prologue

"Weaving Your Tapestry" is more than just a book; it's an invitation. An invitation to explore the depths of your imagination, to harness the power of your thoughts, and to patiently craft the life you deserve. Through a blend of poignant quotes and practical advice, this book empowers you to turn your dreams into reality."

1. Index

2. Art of your words

Art of your words

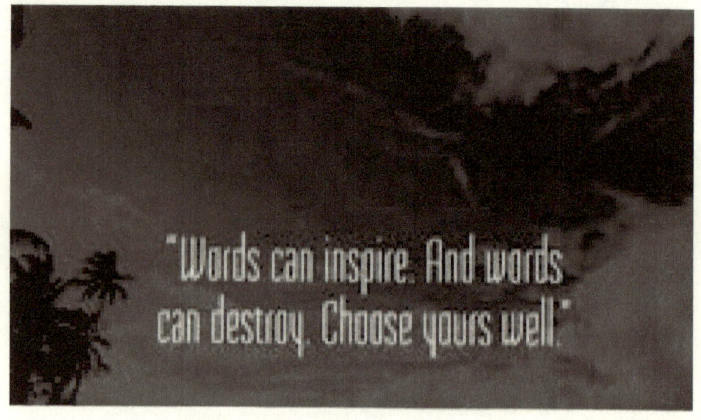

Your words can Heal or destroy some one

Words, like seeds,

can sow both hope and fear,

Nurture dreams or silence every cheer.

A gentle touch, a healing balm,

Or a stinging dart, a cruelest calm.

So choose your words with care and grace,

A kinder world, a better place. Let kindness flow,

let love endure, And mend the hearts, forever pure.

3. Play

Remember words plays important role in describing your image.

People can forget any thing but words take their place in mind and in someone's heart.

4. Words: Your Work's Best Friend or Worst Enemy

"Words can either make your work easy or can make it more difficult".

Words: Your Work's Best Friend or Worst Enemy

Kind words, spoken with sincerity, can have a profound impact on those around us. A simple expression of gratitude, a heartfelt apology, or a word of encouragement can brighten someone's day and strengthen relationships.

By choosing our words carefully, we can create a more positive and harmonious environment. A positive attitude and a kind heart can help us navigate even the most challenging situations.

Remember, words have the power to both heal and harm. Let's use them to uplift and inspire, rather than to tear down and destroy.

5. Inner peace

"when things and people are destroying your inner peace stay a part from them ."

When negative influences threaten your inner peace, it's essential to create distance. This doesn't mean complete isolation, but rather a strategic retreat. By limiting your interactions and sharing fewer personal thoughts, you can safeguard your mental well-being.

Toxic individuals often thrive on drama and negativity. By minimizing your exposure to their influence, you can reduce the impact of their behavior on your life. This allows you to focus on positive relationships and activities that nurture your soul. Remember, prioritizing your mental health is a form of self-care, and it's essential for overall well-being.

6. Character

" <u>Your words forms your character</u> "

Our words are more than just sounds; they are the building blocks of our character. Every word we utter shapes our identity and influences the world around us.

By choosing our words carefully, we can cultivate positive relationships, inspire others, and create a more harmonious world. Let us strive to speak with kindness, empathy, and truth, for our words have the power to heal or harm.

The Erosion of Trust: A Wordy World

In the annals of history, words were considered precious commodities, more valuable than gold or power. A person's identity was often defined by their speech. Trust was a cornerstone of human interaction, a bond forged through honest communication.

However, in our modern world, trust seems to be a diminishing resource. People often engage in double-dealing, speaking differently to different individuals. This duplicity, or "two-sided words," has eroded the foundation of trust.

In a society obsessed with success and status, people often use others as stepping stones. They may feign friendship and loyalty, only to backstab and gossip behind closed doors. This betrayal of trust can have devastating consequences, damaging relationships and fostering a climate of suspicion.

To rebuild trust, we must prioritize honesty, integrity, and empathy. We must strive to be people of our word, who speak with sincerity and kindness. By fostering open and honest communication, we can create a world where trust is once again a valuable currency.

7. wise

A word, a thought,
a fleeting breath, Can sow the seeds of life or death.
Be wise in speech, a careful art,
A gentle touch, a noble heart.
Each word, a brushstroke, paints the scene,
A masterpiece, or a tragic dream.
So choose them well, with mindful care,
A legacy of love, beyond compare.

Power

"Words hold immense power. It's essential to use them wisely and with kindness. One of my colleagues is a great example of this. Regardless of their position or the situation, they always communicate with politeness and positivity. Even when facing challenges, they maintain a calm and respectful demeanor.

True power doesn't come from insulting others. Successful individuals often demonstrate humility and gratitude, rather than resorting to harsh language. Negative words can have lasting consequences, both for the speaker and the recipient.

When faced with insults, responding with dignity and restraint can be more impactful. By not reciprocating negativity, you can leave the other person feeling remorseful and guilty about their behavior. Engaging in a verbal altercation, however, can lead to a cycle of negativity and harm."

8. Mirror

Your words are a mirror to your soul, reflecting your thoughts, beliefs, and character.

-fatema kapadia "

ART OF MIRRORING

The Art of Mirroring: Understanding the Intentions Behind Imitation

When someone mirrors your behaviour and words, it can be attributed to one of two possible reasons. By paying attention to their actions, you can discern their true intentions.

Situation 1: Genuine Admiration

If someone is mirroring you, it's likely because they admire certain qualities you possess. People are naturally drawn to positive traits, and being liked for who you are can be a tremendous confidence booster. Being a role model for someone can also enhance your reputation and self-esteem.

On the other hand, someone might mirror your behaviour to make you feel comfortable or to gain favour. To identify this motive, observe their reactions when you express imperfect or questionable opinions. If they condone or imitate your flaws, it may be a tactic to manipulate your emotions or to flatter you. Be cautious in such situations, as this behaviour can be a sign of opportunism.

Discerning the Difference

To distinguish between genuine admiration and manipulation, pay attention to the following:

1. Consistency: Do their actions align with their words?

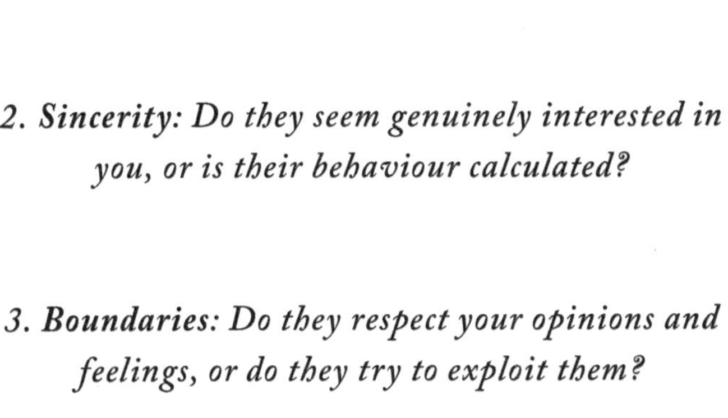

2. Sincerity: Do they seem genuinely interested in you, or is their behaviour calculated?

3. Boundaries: Do they respect your opinions and feelings, or do they try to exploit them?

The Shadow Side of Success

As you ascend the ladder of success, you may find yourself surrounded by those who seek to mirror your achievements. While some may be genuine admirers, others may have ulterior motives. Be cautious of those who imitate your actions or opinions, as they may be seeking personal gain or validation.

Understanding the motivations behind such behavior is crucial. By recognizing the difference between genuine admiration and calculated imitation, you can protect yourself from potential manipulation and maintain your authenticity.

9. Art of thinking

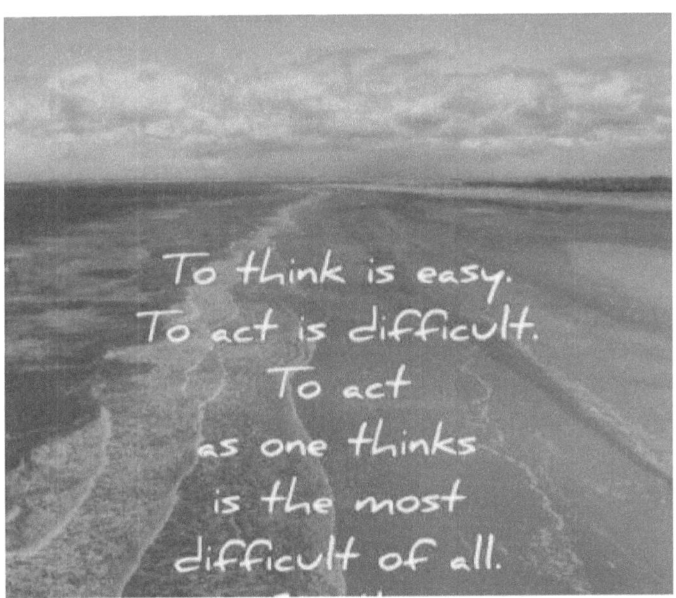

الحمدالله

الحمدالله

For your peace of mind , dont try to understand everything .
Just trust that

what meant for you will always find you , even when you cant
see the path ahead.

In every hardship , there is a lesson and with every trail, there is
ease, so be greateful .

Trust the process , for god wisdom is greater than our
understanding .

you may not know the next chapter , but you know the author .

Trust Him.

10. Choice

> "Every choice we make will either impact us positively or it can seriously have a negative affect on you. Choices are everything, you just have to be careful as to which one is going to help you or hurt you."

11. Impact of negative thoughts

House

"Your mind is your house if house is negative the power of thinking will be that too ".

-fatema kapadia

Taking Risks

Our thoughts have a profound impact on our lives, including our financial well-being. Negative thinking can hinder our progress by limiting our willingness to take risks.

Risk-taking is an essential component of growth. By stepping outside of our comfort zones, we open ourselves up to new opportunities and experiences. However, negative thoughts can paralyze us, preventing us from taking the necessary steps to achieve our goals.

To overcome this, we must cultivate a positive mindset. By focusing on our strengths, visualizing success, and embracing challenges, we can unlock our full potential. Remember, growth often occurs on the other side of fear.

Breaking the Chains

Negativity, a creeping vine,

Envelops hearts, a somber sign.

It casts a doubt, a chilling fear,

Weakening faith, year after year.

A darkened lens, a clouded sight,

Distorting truth, obscuring light.

The gentle hand, the loving grace,

Forgotten now, in this bleak space.

Yet, hope endures, a flicker's gleam,

A whisper soft, a distant dream.

Let's break the chains, dispel the night,

Embrace the dawn, with all our might.

For faith, a gift, a sacred art, Must rise above, with hopeful heart.

Let positivity's warm rays unfold,

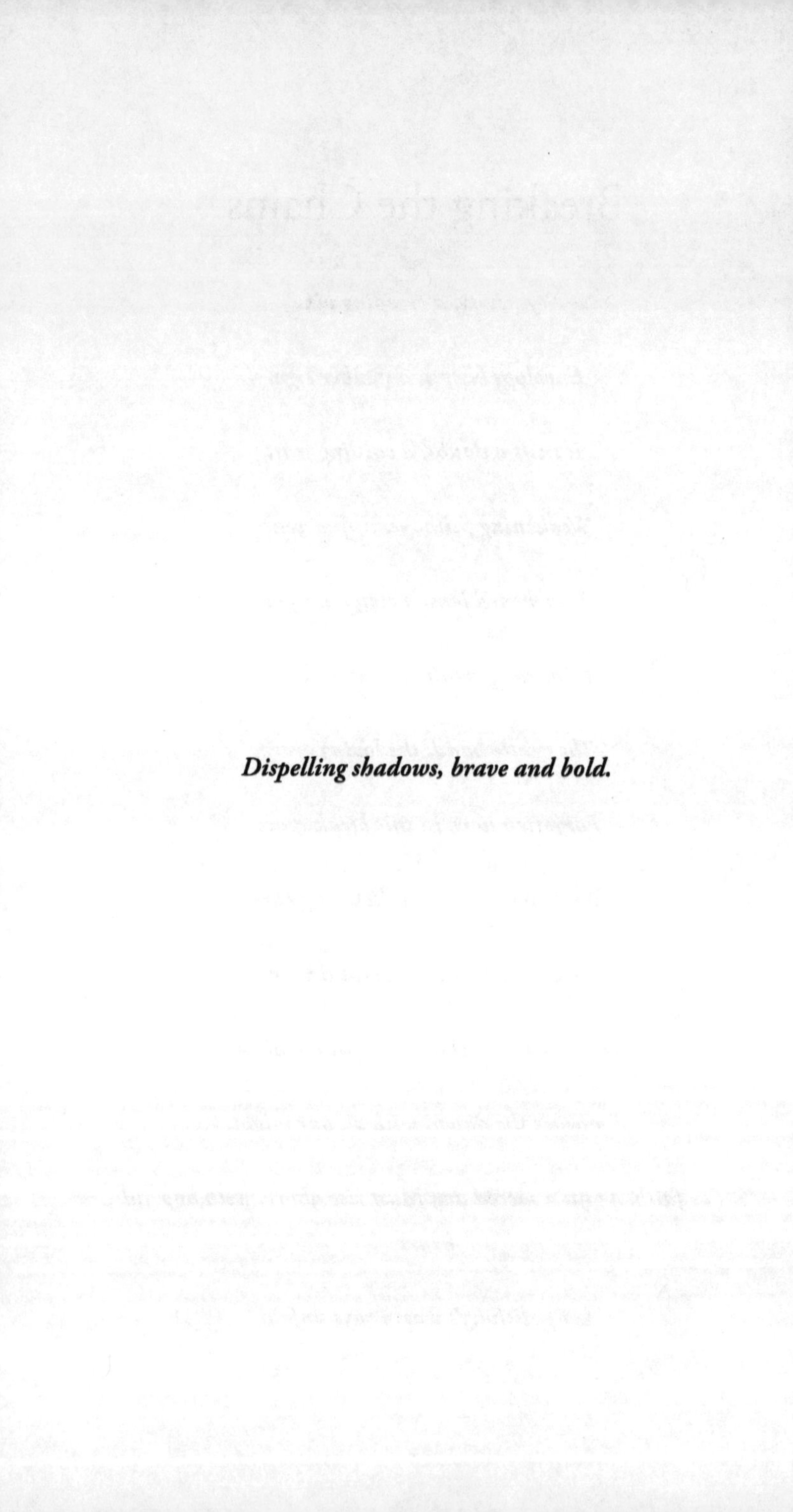

Dispelling shadows, brave and bold.

Impact

Negative thoughts impact on taking risk .

Risk indicate the trust on God.

If you trust on God then negativity don't have place .

If the density is all planned by god himself then why you stop your self from growing..?

Negativity, a darkened cloud,

Negativity, a darkened cloud,

Casts shadows long, a somber shroud.

It stirs the mind, a troubled sea,

Breeding discontent, wild and free.

In love's embrace, a fragile art,

Negative thoughts tear us apart.

A single seed, a growing fear,

Nurturing doubt, year after year.

Depressed and weary, spirits low,

A heavy burden, hard to know.

But let us rise, with hopeful heart,

And choose the light, a brand new start

12. Thoughts

"A negativity thoughts can lead you to Self sabotaging behaviour and procrastination"

Self-sabotaging

Self-sabotaging behaviour refers to actions or inactions

that hinder one's success or prevent the achievement of goals.

self-sabotaging

Negative thinking can lead to self-sabotaging behavior. Success often hinges on taking risks.

As the saying goes, 'If you never fall, you'll never learn to rise.'

And in those moments of falling, you'll truly discover who stands by you, both in success and failure."

13. Procrastination

"DON'T LET
PROCRASTINATION
TAKE OVER
YOUR LIFE.
BE BRAVE
AND TAKE RISKS.
YOUR LIFE IS
HAPPENING
RIGHT NOW."

Procrastination

Procrastination means delaying the process or work due to lack of motivation, fear of failure or lack of decision making process.

Negative Thinking, Delayed Action

Negative thinking may cause Procrastination .

When people often fall in negativity they delay there works

which causes negative impact on there works , deadline etc ..

Negative thinking can be a significant contributor to procrastination. When individuals frequently engage in negative self-talk, they often find themselves delaying tasks and avoiding challenges. This pattern of behavior can have a detrimental impact on productivity, work quality, and overall well-being.

How Negative Thinking Fuels Procrastination:

Fear of Failure: Negative thoughts can lead to a fear of failure, making individuals hesitant to start a task. They may worry about making mistakes, not meeting expectations, or being judged negatively.

Low Self-Esteem: Negative self-talk can erode self-esteem, making individuals doubt their abilities. They may believe that they are not capable of completing tasks successfully, leading to procrastination.

Perfectionism: Negative thinking can lead to perfectionist tendencies, where individuals set unrealistic standards for themselves. They may fear that their work is not good enough, leading to endless revisions and delays.

Overwhelm: When faced with a challenging task, negative thinking can magnify the perceived difficulty. Individuals may feel overwhelmed and unable to cope, leading to procrastination as a coping mechanism.

Avoidance of Discomfort: Negative emotions associated with a task, such as boredom or anxiety, can motivate individuals to avoid it altogether. Procrastination becomes a way to escape these unpleasant feelings.

Navigating Life's Lessons and Changes

Throughout our lives, we encounter a diverse range of people, each leaving an imprint on our journey. Some provide valuable lessons, shaping our understanding of the world, while others catalyze significant transformations, altering the course of our lives.

The choice to embrace these lessons and changes is ultimately ours. By acknowledging the importance of both, we can grow and evolve as individuals. Some experiences teach us valuable life skills and moral values, while others necessitate significant shifts in our perspectives or behaviors.

By embracing both lessons and changes, we can become better versions of ourselves.

Example

A person with a negative mindset often struggles to perceive positive aspects of life. A classic example is the half-full glass of water. While an optimistic person sees the glass as half full, a negative thinker focuses on the empty half. Similarly, negative individuals tend to fixate on the flaws and mistakes of others, neglecting to appreciate their inner qualities. This can significantly impact social relationships, as constant complaining and judgment can alienate others. Such individuals may also be resistant to advice and feedback, hindering personal growth."

14. The Root of Negative Thinking

Negative thoughts often stem from feelings of dissatisfaction and insecurity. When we compare ourselves to others, we risk falling into a cycle of self-doubt and negativity. It's important to recognize that everyone's journey is unique, and comparing ourselves to others can be a harmful practice.

To cultivate a positive mindset, we must focus on our own strengths and accomplishments. By practicing gratitude, mindfulness, and self-compassion, we can overcome negative thinking and embrace a more fulfilling life.

15. A Tale of Two Worlds

Once upon a time, in the heart of Europe, lived a contented farmer. His land was lush, his crops abundant, and his spirit was light. A serene pond mirrored the beauty of the surrounding countryside, adding to the tranquility of his existence.

One day, a visitor from across the Atlantic arrived. This man, hailing from the bustling cities of America, observed the farmer's simple life and offered a critical assessment. "You have a farm, a house, and a pond," he remarked, "but you lack diamonds, cars, and great wealth. You toil endlessly, yet your rewards are modest."

The farmer, initially unperturbed, gradually began to internalize these words. A seed of doubt was sown in his mind. He started to question the value of his simple life, comparing it to the opulent lifestyles he had seen in the movies and magazines.

As the days turned into weeks, the farmer's once-positive outlook began to dim. He neglected his fields, his mind consumed by fantasies of riches and luxury. The pond, once a source of solace, now reflected his growing discontent.

In the end, the farmer's dreams of a lavish lifestyle overshadowed his practical reality. His crops withered, his livestock dwindled, and his once-peaceful existence was shattered. The visitor's well-intentioned advice had inadvertently led to the farmer's downfall.

This tale serves as a poignant reminder of the dangers of comparing oneself to others. The farmer's happiness and success were rooted in his simple, fulfilling life. However, the allure of material possessions and societal expectations led him astray.

It is essential to recognize the value of our own unique circumstances and to cultivate gratitude for what we have. While it's important to strive for improvement, we must also learn to appreciate the present moment. By focusing on our strengths and passions, we can achieve true fulfillment and contentment.

As the wise saying goes, "The grass is always greener on the other side." But it's often just a trick of the light.

16. The Power of positivity

A Sunlit Soul

A sunbeam's kiss, a hopeful sigh,

A flicker of joy, a reason to try.

A heart that's light, a spirit unbound,

In positivity's embrace, peace is found.

A gentle breeze, a calming sight,

A beacon of hope, a guiding light.

A smile that spreads, a laugh that's true,

In positivity's embrace, dreams come anew.

A grateful heart, a thankful mind,

A future so bright, a hope enshrined.

A steadfast soul, a resilient will,

In positivity's embrace, life's mountain's hill.

Unleash the Power Within

"If you think positive you attitude will be same ".

A positive mindset can significantly impact our lives. When we choose to focus on the positive aspects of a situation, we invite optimism, hope, and resilience. This positive outlook can lead to increased motivation, better problem-solving skills, and stronger relationships

Precious Gift

Positivity's a gift, a precious sight,

A beacon shining, ever pure and bright.

A treasure trove, within your soul it gleams,

Dispelling shadows, chasing darkest dreams.

It costs no coin, no wealth, no worldly gain,

Yet priceless treasure, easing every pain.

A simple choice, a mindset, pure and free,

To paint your world with hues of joy and glee.

So let it shine, this gift, so rare and fine,

A radiant beacon, eternally divine.

A choice to make, a path to boldly tread,

Embrace positivity, lift your weary head.

A Positive Mind, A Victor's Might

A Positive Mind, A Victor's Might

A mind aflame, with hope's bright fire,

A spirit soaring, reaching ever higher.

A heart that beats, with courage bold and true,

A soul that shines, a radiant, hopeful hue.

For in this mind, a universe resides,

A realm of dreams, where hope abides.

A canvas vast, where thoughts take flight,

Painting visions, bathed in morning light.

No foe can match, no challenge can withstand,

The power of a positive, determined hand.

A mind that's strong, a will that's pure,

Conquering obstacles, forevermore secure.

Bounce Back Stronger

While a person with a positive mindset may still experience failures, they possess the unique ability to rebound from setbacks with renewed vigor. Their positive outlook empowers them to learn from mistakes, adapt to challenges, and ultimately emerge stronger than before.

Rise Above

Positive thinkers aren't naive; they understand the intentions of those who try to bring them down. Despite this knowledge, they choose to maintain a positive outlook and focus on their goals. This positive mindset empowers them to overcome obstacles and achieve success.

Shadows

No naivete, their eyes see clear,

The shadows cast, the motives drear.

Yet, hope's bright flame within them burns,

A steadfast heart, a lesson learned.

They climb the heights, with spirit bold,

Unwavering, their story told.

A positive mind, a powerful shield,

Defying darkness, a brighter field.

With every step, a victory won,

A testament to what can be done.

So let us learn, from their wise art,

To nurture hope, and mend the heart.

Ignoring the Naysayer

As you climb the ladder towards your dreams, you'll encounter a sea of naysayers who doubt your path to success. However, truly successful individuals rise above this negativity, ignoring the noise and focusing on their goals. They overcome setbacks and emerge stronger, proving that perseverance and a positive mindset are key to achieving greatness.

A naysayer is a person who habitually expresses negative or pessimistic views.

17. Path

A ladder ascends, a dream takes flight,
A path less trodden, bathed in light.
Yet voices rise, a chorus of doubt,
A sea of negativity, all about.
But heed them not, the chosen few,
With hearts aflame, and spirits true.
They rise above, with steadfast will,
Conquering obstacles, hill by hill.
Perseverance, their guiding star,
A positive mind, reaching ever far.
They silence the noise, the critics' creed,
And carve their destiny, a noble deed.

The Power of Perseverance

Many successful people, from renowned entrepreneurs to celebrated artists, didn't start with a silver spoon. They didn't inherit wealth or privilege. Instead, they built their empires brick by brick, facing numerous setbacks and failures along the way.

A prime example is J.K. Rowling, the author of the Harry Potter series. Before her monumental success, she was a struggling single mother, rejected by numerous publishers. However, she persevered, believing in her vision. Her determination and positive attitude ultimately led to the creation of one of the most beloved book series of all time.

Another inspiring figure is Elon Musk. His ventures, such as Tesla and SpaceX, have revolutionized industries. But Musk's journey has been filled with challenges, including product failures and financial difficulties. Yet, he has consistently bounced back, fueled by his unwavering belief in innovation and his relentless pursuit of ambitious goals.

These examples highlight the importance of embracing failure as a learning opportunity. It's not about avoiding setbacks but about how we respond to them. By refusing to let failures define us, we can harness their power to propel us forward.

success stories

True success stories, often untold,

Arise from struggle, valiant and bold.

Not birthed from fortune, nor silver spoon,

But forged in the fire, beneath the moon.

Countless attempts, failures endured,

Lessons learned, spirits assured.

Fear, a foe to be bravely faced,

Pride in the fall, a noble grace.

So let's embrace missteps,

each one a guide, A stepping stone, a reason to stride.

For in the heart of failure, strength resides,

A catalyst for dreams, a future that abides.

Ashes of your failures.

Our successes are often born from the ashes of your failures. Without experiencing setbacks, you can't truly understand your resilience and strength.

Rise from the Ashes

From ashes rise,

a phoenix's flight, Success takes form,

bathed in morning light.

For in each fall, a lesson's seed is sown,

A stronger spirit, a heart well-known.

No victory's pure, no triumph's free,

From trials endured, true strength we see.

Resilience forged, in failure's fire,

A testament to unwavering desire.

Stepping stones

"When you're climbing the ladder of success, you'll encounter a sea of people who'll doubt your path. But successful individuals rise above negativity, transforming failures into stepping stones to greatness."

Fear not failure, embrace it

Success stories aren't fairy tales handed down by wealthy parents. They're gritty narratives, etched with the marks of countless trials and heart-wrenching failures.

Fear not failure, embrace it. Let it be your mentor, your guide, and your greatest teacher. For it is in the crucible of adversity that true strength is forged. Remember, every setback is a setup for a comeback.

As the adage wisely states, "Success is derived from failure." Without experiencing the sting of defeat, how can you truly appreciate the sweetness of victory? Each failure is a stepping stone, leading you closer to your ultimate goal.

So, dare to dream, dare to fail, and dare to rise again. The world is yours to conquer, one challenge at a time

A Road to Greatness

The path to greatness is long and tough,

No easy road, no lucky bluff.

With every stumble, a lesson's learned,

A chance to grow, a spirit burned.

Don't fear the fall, the slip, the slide,

For in the darkness, strength will abide.

Embrace the challenge, the uphill climb,

And rise above, defying time.

Success is born from failure's might,

A paradox, a puzzling sight. Without the storm,

no rainbow's hue, Without the struggle, victory's few.

So let us strive, with all our might,

To reach the stars, and shine so bright.

For in the end, it's not the goal,

But the journey's worth, that makes us whole.

18. Art of patience

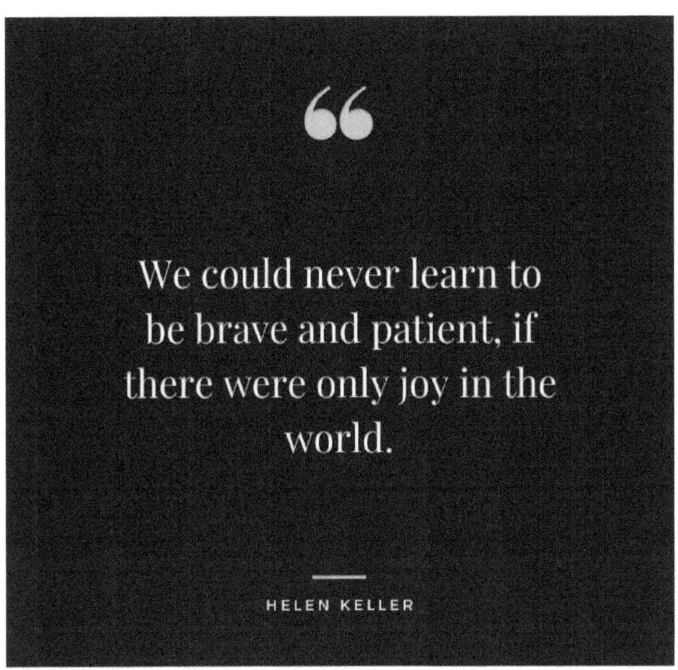

Patience - Good quality

Patience is a good quality that many people don't think is important. It's about being calm and not getting angry when things don't go your way or take longer than you'd like.

Real patience isn't just giving up; it's about choosing to be calm and accepting the situation, even if it's tough. It's about waiting, but not just sitting around. It's about being hopeful and believing that good things will happen, even when things seem bad.

In today's world, we often want things right away. Patience helps us stay calm and think before we act. It helps us deal with problems in a good way.

Remember, being patient isn't about giving up. It's about keeping going, even when it's hard. It's about believing in yourself and trusting that things will work out in the end.

A beautiful quality

Patience is a beautiful quality that helps us stay calm and composed, even when things get tough. It means being able to accept delays, difficulties, and annoyances without getting upset or complaining.

Think of it like this: Imagine you're waiting in a long line. You could get frustrated and impatient, or you could use that time to relax, read a book, or simply enjoy the moment. Choosing the latter is an act of patience.

Patience is not about giving up or being weak. It's about being strong enough to endure challenges with a peaceful mind. It's about trusting the process and believing that good things will come in time.

So, next time you find yourself facing a difficult situation, remember the power of patience. It can help you navigate life's challenges with grace and resilience.

A Patient Heart

No passive spirit, weak or slow,

A heart serene, a steady glow.

Trusting the process, the grand design,

A patient soul, both strong and fine.

-fatema kapadia .

Shields

Awaiting calmly, serene and still,

A heart that's patient, steadfast will.

No fretting, no fear, no anxious sigh,

A peaceful soul, reaching for the sky.

A gift divine, a treasure rare,

Patience's power, beyond compare.

It soothes the soul, a gentle balm,

Shields from life's storms, a sacred calm

-fatema kapadia.

A Breath of Patience

To breathe when skies are gray and tight,

A steady heart, a guiding light.

To weather storms, serene and strong,

Endure the night, and right the wrong.

A patient soul, a steadfast mind,

A quiet strength, of peaceful kind.

Emerging brighter, stronger, pure,

A testament to hope, forever sure.

A Patient Heart, A Warrior's Soul

A person with a positive mindset possesses a remarkable quality: patience. They understand that good things take time and are willing to wait, no matter how long it may seem. They are not swayed by the opinions of others, staying steadfast in their belief and purpose.

Patience is often mistaken for weakness, but it's quite the opposite. A patient person is a strong individual, a true warrior. They possess the inner strength to endure challenges, the resilience to bounce back from setbacks, and the wisdom to understand that timing is everything.

A Moment of Patience

Frustration's grip, a fleeting sight,

A test of will, a darkened night.

Yet, wisdom whispers, soft and clear,

Greatness unfolds, year after year.

So let us wait, with hopeful heart,

For dreams to bloom, a work of art.

Time, the sculptor, shapes with care,

A masterpiece, beyond compare.

Meaning

Weaving Your Tapestry: Unleashing Your Inner Creator

Meaning:

This phrase invites you to view your life as a work of art, a tapestry that you are actively creating. Just like a weaver carefully selects and interweaves threads to create a beautiful pattern, you have the power to shape your own destiny through your thoughts, actions, and choices.

Unleashing your inner creator means tapping into your innate creativity and potential. It involves:

<u>Embracing your individuality</u>: Recognizing your unique talents and skills.

Cultivating a positive mindset: Fostering a belief in yourself and your abilities.

Taking inspired action: Turning your ideas and dreams into reality.

Connecting with your intuition: Listening to your inner voice and trusting your instincts.

By embracing your inner creator, you can live a more fulfilling and meaningful life. You can overcome challenges, achieve your goals, and create a legacy that inspires others.

A Final Thought

As you embark on your journey of self-discovery and creativity, remember that the power to shape your own destiny lies within you. By nurturing your inner creator, you can weave a tapestry of life that is uniquely yours.

May this book inspire you to:

<u>Embrace your individuality:</u> Celebrate your unique talents and perspectives.

<u>Cultivate a positive mindset:</u> Nurture optimism and resilience.

<u>Take inspired action:</u> Turn your dreams into reality.

<u>Connect with your higher self:</u> *Tap into your inner wisdom and intuition.*

Remember, the journey of self-discovery is a lifelong adventure. May you continue to explore, create, and evolve.

Thank you for reading.

If you have enjoyed this book, please consider leaving a review. Your feedback helps us continue to create inspiring content.

CHANAKYA
THE CAREER SARTHI

WINNING WORK LIFE

Scan me to view
author's profile now

SHREY SAO, CFA

INDIA · SINGAPORE · MALAYSIA